Traditional Nova Scotian Double-Knitting Patterns

Janetta Dexter

Nimbus Publishing and
The Nova Scotia Museum
Halifax, Nova Scotia
1993

93 94 95 96 97 98 99 8 7 6 5 4 3 2

Produced as part of the Nova Scotia Museum Program of the Department of Education, Province of Nova Scotia

Minister: The Hon. Guy J. Le Blanc
Deputy Minister: Armand F. Pinard

Co-published by Nimbus Publishing Limited
and the Nova Scotia Museum

A product of the
Nova Scotia Government Co-publishing Program

Designed by the
Nova Scotia Museum

Produced by the
Department of Government Services

Canadian Cataloguing in Publication Data

Dexter, Janetta.
Traditional Nova Scotian double-knitting patterns
(Peeper)

Co-published by the Nova Scotia Museum.
ISBN 0-919680-29-1

1. Knitting—Nova Scotia—Patterns. I. Title.
II. Nova Scotia Museum. III. Series.

TT820.D49 1992 746.43'2041 C85-085498-9

Contents

Introduction

In the summer of 1972, Janetta Dexter was asked to demonstrate knitting at the Western Nova Scotia Arts and Crafts Association's demonstration and sale as part of B.A.S.H., the Centennial Celebration of Bridgetown. She knitted a pair of mittens in a double-knitting pattern she had learned from her grandmother and displayed some other articles in bi-colour patterns. During the demonstration, she collected several other patterns from ladies who stopped to chat. It became obvious to her that each of these women knew only one or two patterns and that each area seemed to have its own patterns, so she began looking for patterns wherever she went.

On a visit to Lunenburg County in the summer of 1973, Janetta found several patterns including the one she called "Maplewood" which she later learned is called "Northern Star."

During the winter of 1973, Janetta's friend Betty Hearn kept prodding her to put her patterns down on paper, together with the directions for knitting them, which she finally did. They were made into a small booklet and sold to Women's Institutes and at the Sheep Fair in Truro where I first met Janetta and saw the lovely articles made from those patterns. I invited Janetta to come to Sherbrooke Village in the fall of 1974 to demonstrate and display her patterns here.

Since the production of the booklet, Janetta has discovered several more designs so we decided an enlarged version was in order.

Polly Greene
Sherbrooke Village
Sherbrooke, N.S.

Author's Note

These patterns are not new. It seems probable that most of them were brought by our ancestors from Great Britain, France and Germany. They knit them in homespun wool in natural shades of black, white and gray or in yarns dyed in soft colours with natural dyes.

The name "Double-Knitting" is used here to mean knitting with two contrasting colours in an all-over pattern in which the thread not in use is carried along on the wrong side of the work. This gives an extra layer of wool in the finsihed work making it doubly warm.

In all the directions, the "D" is used for the dark yarn and "L" for the light one.

Janetta Dexter
Hampton, Annapolis Co.,
Nova Scotia

Betty's Wallpaper

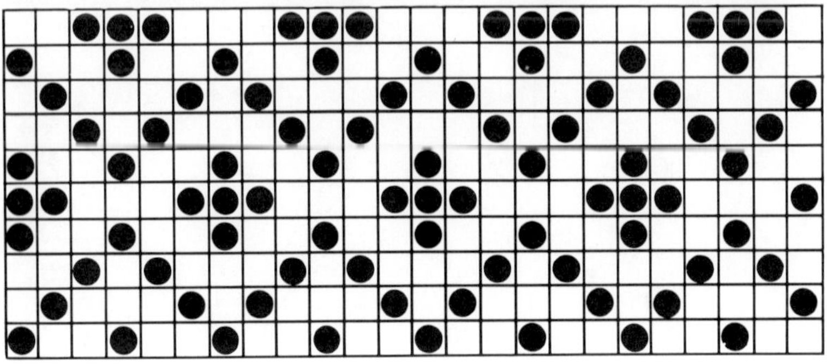

This is a pattern which I made based on the design of Betty Hearn's wallpaper. It is knit in a multiple of twelve stitches.

Row 1: k 2L, (3D, 3L)*, 3D, 1L
Row 2: k (1D, 2L)*
Row 3: k 1L, 1D, (3L, 1D, 1L, 1D)*, 3L, 1D
Row 4: k 2L, (1D, 1L, 1D, 3L)*, 1D, 1L, 1D, 1L
Row 5: Same as Row 2
Row 6: k 2D, (3L, 3D)*, 3L, 1D
Row 7: Same as Row 2
Row 8: Same as Row 4
Row 9: Same as Row 3
Row 10: Same as Row 2

Broken Stripes

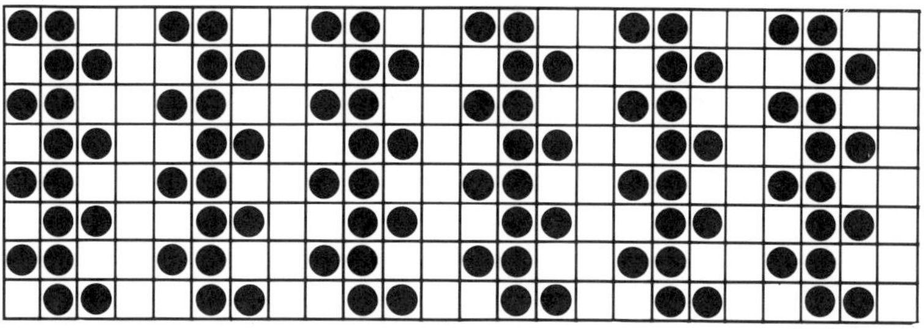

This was the first and easiest double-knit pattern I learned. It was taught to me by my grandmother when I was living in Lunenburg County. It is knit in a multiple of four stitches.

Row 1: k (2D, 2L)*
Row 2: k 1L, (2D, 2L)*, 2D, 1L

These two rows form the pattern. For flat pieces, purl Row 2 reading the color sequence in reverse on this row.

Candlelit Windows

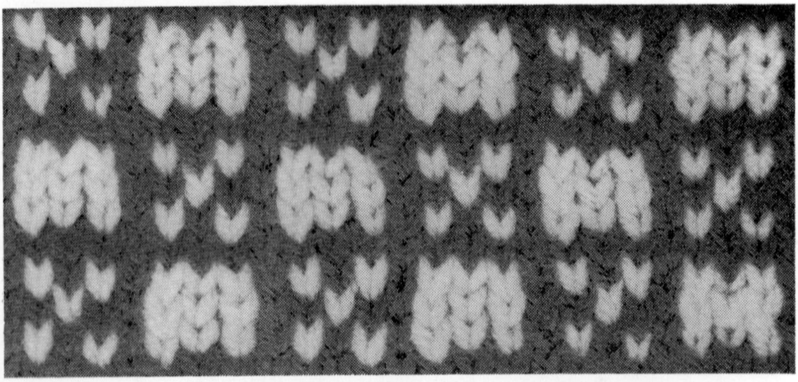

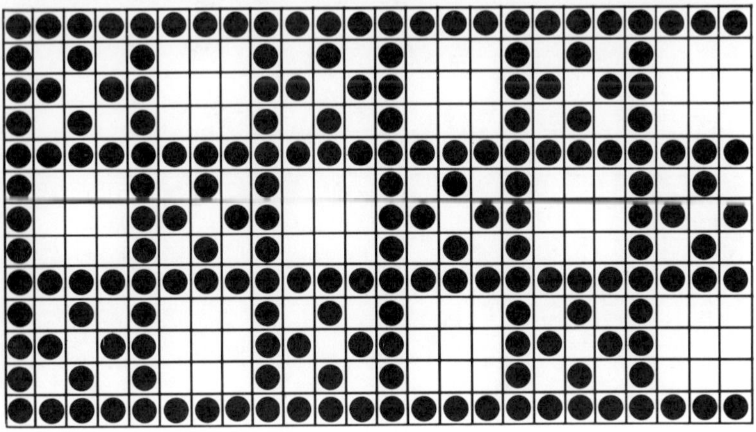

A very dainty pattern, knit in a multiple of four stitches (plus one for flat pieces).

Row 1: k D
Row 2: k (1D, 1L, 1D, 1L, 1D, 3L)*
Row 3: k (2D, 1L, 2D, 3L)*
Row 4: Same as Row 2
Row 5: k D
Row 6: k (1D, 3L, 1D, 1L, 1D, 1L)*
Row 7: k (1D, 3L, 2D, 1L, 1D)*
Row 8: Same as Row 6

For flat pieces, purl all even numbered rows, color sequence unchanged.

Checkerboard

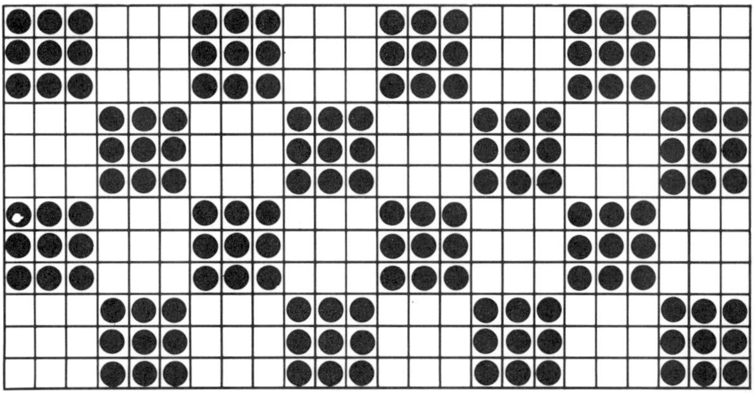

While this pattern is shown in a multiple of three stitches, it may be knit in larger blocks or in a multiple of two.

Rows 1, 2 and 3: k (3D, 3L)*
Rows 4, 5 and 6: k (3L, 3D)*

These directions are for knitting in the round. For flat knitting purl Rows 2, 4 and 6, color sequence unchanged.

Diamond and Fleur-de-lis

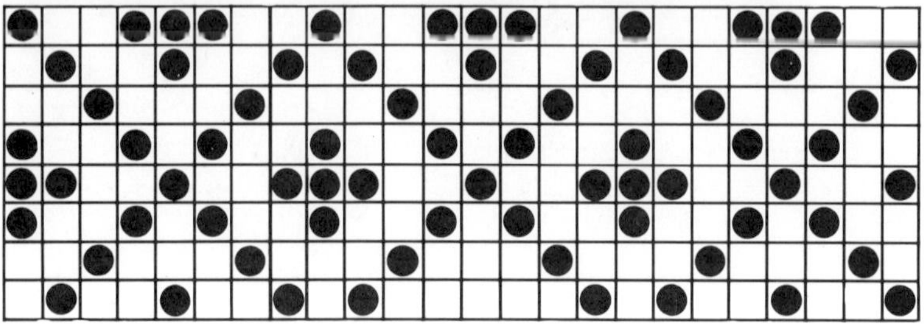

A combination of two old patterns which is much more effective than either alone. Knit in a multiple of eight stitches.

Row 1: k (1D, 2L, 3D, 2L)*
Row 2: k (1L, 1D, 2L, 1D, 2L, 1D)*
Row 3: k 2L, (1D, 3L)*, 1D, 1L
Row 4: k (1D, 2L, 1D, 1L, 1D, 2L)*
Row 5: k (2D, 2L, 1D, 2L, 1D)*
Row 6: Same as Row 4
Row 7: Same as Row 3
Row 8: Same as Row 2

Diamond Variant

This pattern is not an old one but one which I adapted from Double Diamond. It is knit in a multiple of sixteen stitches.

Rows 1 & 2: k 3D, (2L, 1D, 2L, 3D)*, 2L, 1D, 2L
Rows 3 & 4: k 1L, 1D, (2L, 3D, 2L, 1D)*, 2L, 3D, 1L
Rows 5 & 6: k (3L, 2D, 1L, 2D)*
Rows 7 & 8: k 1D, 1L, (2D, 3L, 2D, 1L)*, 2D, 3L, 1D
Rows 9 to 12: Repeat Rows 1 to 4
Rows 13 & 14: Same as 1 & 2
Rows 15 & 16: Same as 7 & 8
Rows 17 & 18: Same as 5 & 6
Rows 19 & 20: Same as 3 & 4

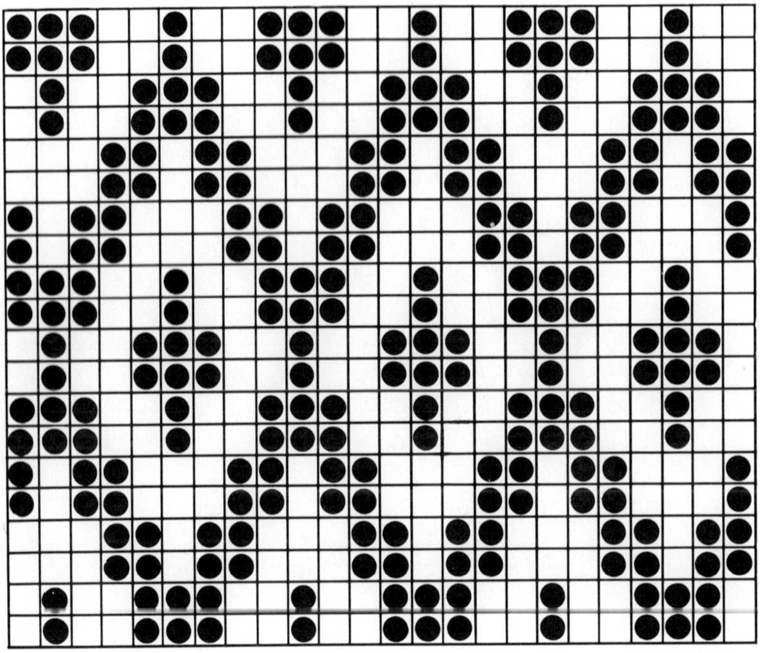

Double Diamond

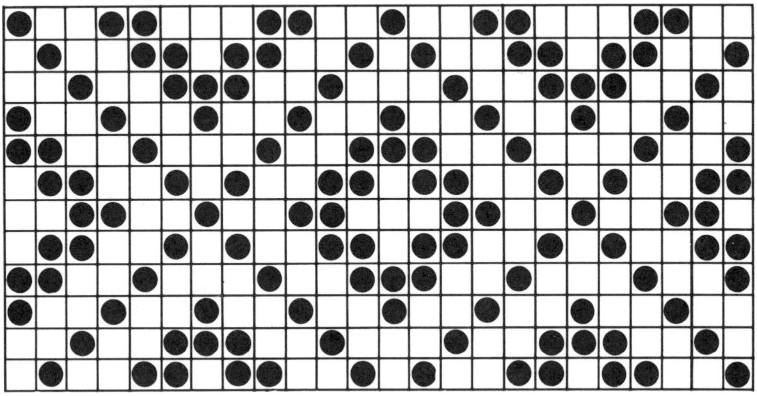

Knit in a multiple of twelve stitches.

Row 1: k (1D, 2L, 2D, 3L, 2D, 2L)*
Row 2: k (1L, 1D, 2L, 2D, 1L, 2D, 2L, 1D)*
Row 3: k (2L, 1D, 2L, 3D, 2L, 1D, 1L)*
Row 4: k (1D, 2L)*
Row 5: k (2D, 2L, 1D, 3L, 1D, 2L, 1D)*
Row 6: k (1L, 2D, 2L, 1D, 1L, 1D, 2L, 2D)*
Row 7: k (2L, 2D, 2L, 1D, 2L, 2D, 1L)*

Row 7 is the centre of the diamond. Knit from Row 6 to Row 2 to complete the pattern.

Flying Geese

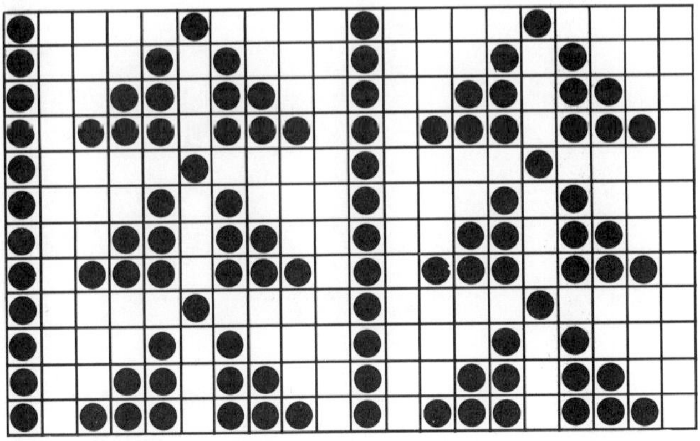

This old pattern was shown to me by Mrs. Murdock Hollingsworth of Truro at the 1974 Sheep Fair. She said that it was traditionally used for gloves with four bands of pattern on the back of the hand. A fifth band is started on the thumb and the pattern is carried to the ends of the thumb and fingers. Knit in a multiple of ten stitches.

Row 1: k (1D, 4L)*
Row 2: k (1D, 3L, 1D, 1L, 1D, 3L)*
Row 3: k (1D, 2L, 2D, 1L, 2D, 2L)*
Row 4: k (1D, 1L, 3D, 1L, 3D, 1L)*

Flying Geese Variant

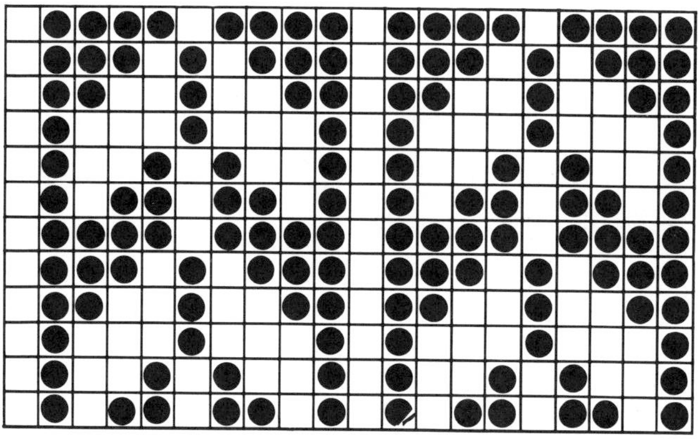

This variant of Flying Geese, like the simpler one on page 11, is said to have been used for gloves with four bands of pattern on the back of the hand and one pattern running up the thumb. I was able to do this only by using a finer yarn than commonly used for double knitting and knitting with no. 14 needles.

Row 1: k (1L, 4D)*, 1L
Row 2: k (1L, 3D, 1L, 1D, 1L, 3D)*, 1L
Row 3: k (1L, 2D, 2L, 1D, 2L, 2D)*, 1L
Row 4: k (1L, 1D, 3L, 1D, 3L, 1D)*, 1L
Row 5: k (1L, 1D, 2L, 1D, 1L, 1D, 2L, 1D)*, 1L
Row 6: k (1L, 1D, 1L, 2D, 1L, 2D, 1L, 1D)*, 1L

Fox and Geese

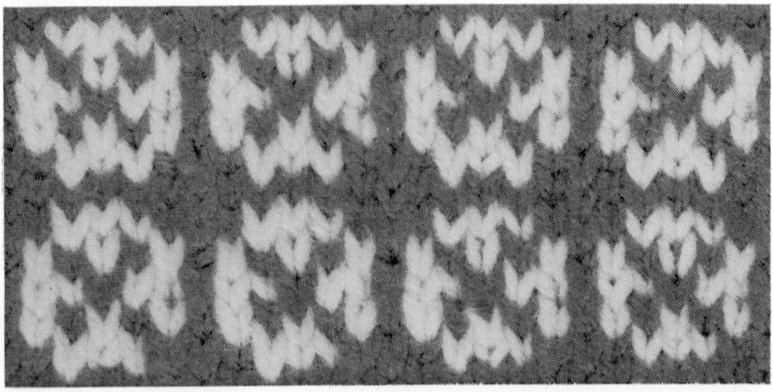

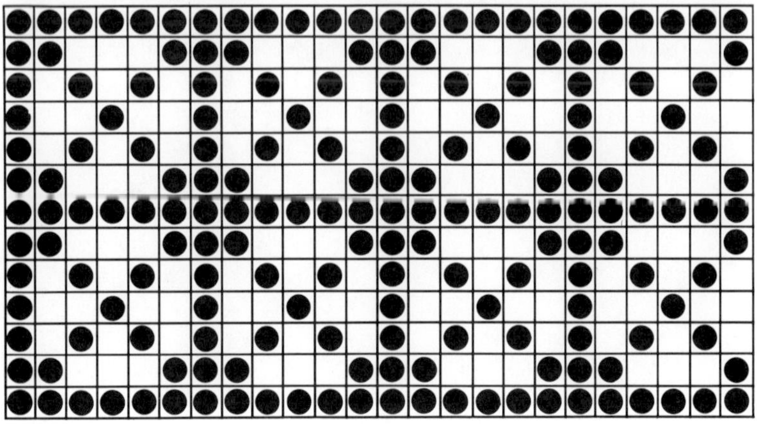

Knit in a multiple of six stitches (plus 1 to balance in flat pieces).

Row 1: k D
Row 2: k 2D, (3L, 3D)*, 3L, 1D
Row 3: k (1D, 1L)*
Row 4: k (1D, 2L)*
Row 5: Same as Row 3
Row 6: Same as Row 2

These directions are for knitting in the round. For flat pieces, purl Rows 2, 4, and 6 making the additional stitch dark, then reading remainder of color sequence from right to left in these rows.

Goose Eye

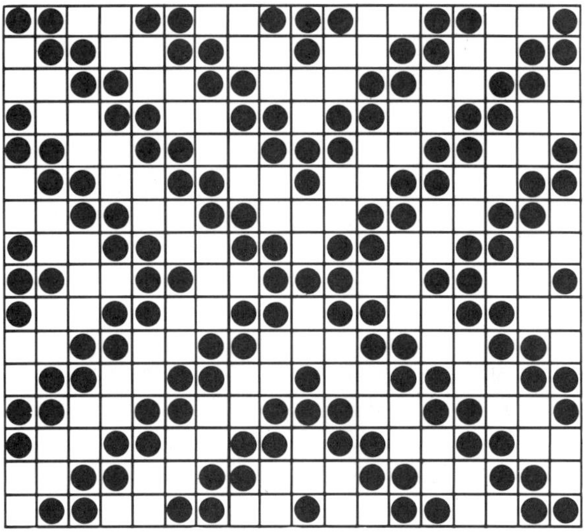

Knit in a multiple of eighteen stitiches.

Row 1: k (2D, 2L, 2D, 2L, 3D, 2L, 2D, 2L, 1D)*
Row 2: k (1L, 2D, 2L, 2D, 2L, 1D, 2L, 2D, 2L, 2D)*
Row 3: k (2L, 2D, 2L, 2D, 3L, 2D, 2L, 2D, 1L)*
Row 4: k (1D, 2L, 2D, 2L, 2D, 1L, 2D, 2L, 2D, 2L)*
Row 5: Same as Row 1
Row 6: Same as Row 2
Row 7: Same as Row 3
Row 8: Same as Row 4
Row 9: Same as Row 1

Knit Rows 8 to 2 in reverse to complete pattern.

Houndstooth

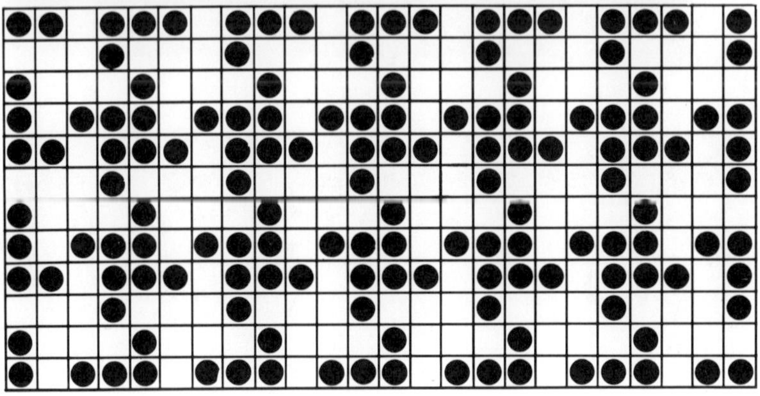

Knit in a multiple of four stitches.

Row 1: k 2D, (1L, 3D)*, 1L, 1D
Row 2: k (3L, 1D)*
Row 3: k (1D, 3L)*
Row 4: k 1D, (1L, 3D)*, 1L, 2D

These directions are for knitting in the round. For flat knitting, purl Rows 2 and 4 reading color sequence from right to left.

Lampshades

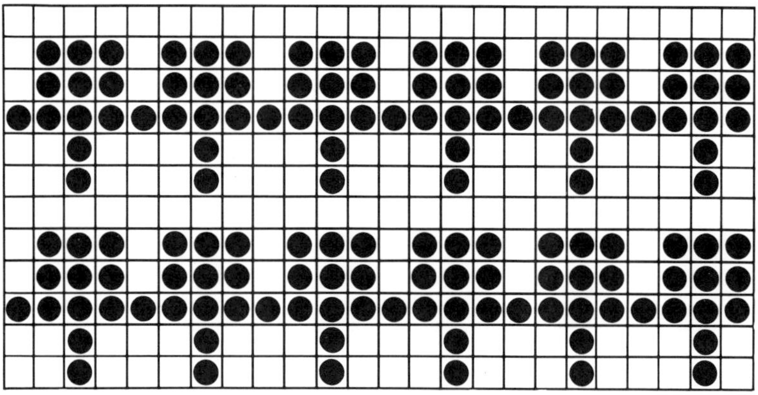

Knit in multiples of eight stitches (plus one for flat pieces).

Row 1: k L
Row 2: k (1L, 3D)*
Row 3: Same as Row 2
Row 4: k D
Row 5: k 2L, (1D, 3L)*, 1D, 1L
Row 6: Same as Row 5

For flat pieces the additional stitch is light in all except Row 3. Purl even-numbered rows reading color sequence from right to left.

Maplewood

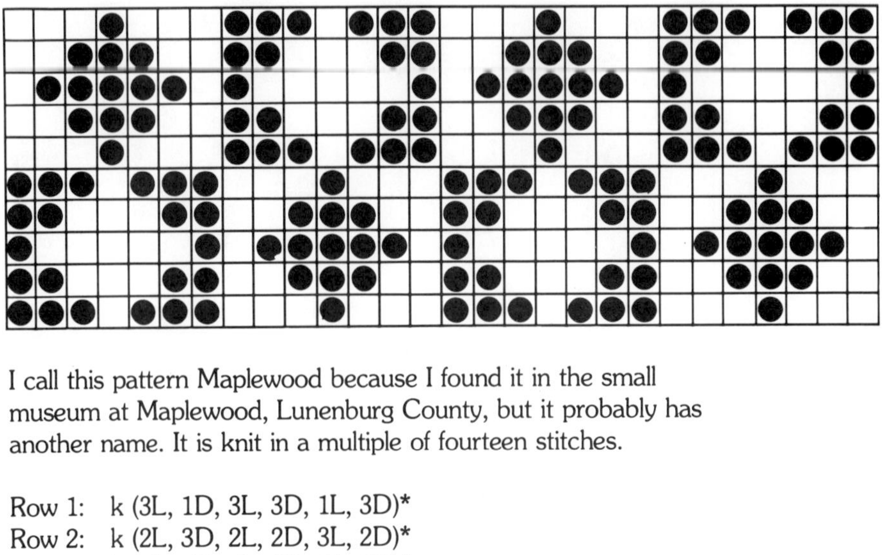

I call this pattern Maplewood because I found it in the small museum at Maplewood, Lunenburg County, but it probably has another name. It is knit in a multiple of fourteen stitches.

Row 1: k (3L, 1D, 3L, 3D, 1L, 3D)*
Row 2: k (2L, 3D, 2L, 2D, 3L, 2D)*
Row 3: k (1L, 5D, 1L, 1D, 5L, 1D)*
Row 4: Same as Row 2
Row 5: Same as Row 1
Row 6: k (3D, 1L, 3D, 3L, 1D, 3L)*
Row 7: k (2D, 3L, 2D, 2L, 3D, 2L)*
Row 8: k (1D, 5L, 1D, 1L, 5D, 1L)*
Row 9: Same as Row 7
Row 10: Same as Row 6

Old German Pattern

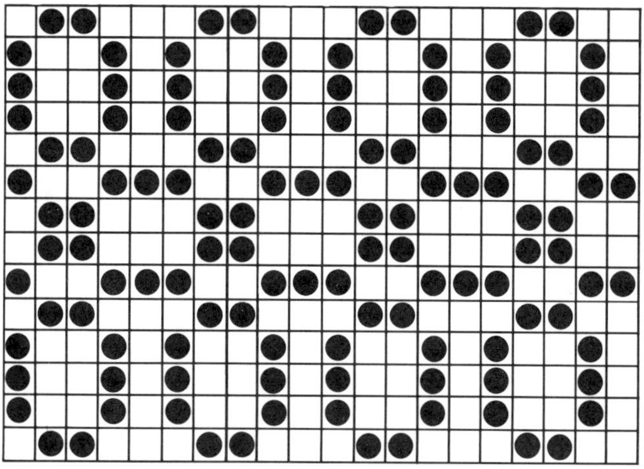

Shown to me by a post-World War II German immigrant at the 1974 Sheep Fair in Truro.

Row 1: k 1L, (2D, 3L)*, 2D, 2L
Row 2: k (1D, 2L, 1D, 1L)*
Row 3: Same as Row 2
Row 4: Same as Row 2
Row 5: Same as Row 1
Row 6: k 1D, (2L, 3D)*, 2L, 2D
Row 7: k 1L, (2D, 3L)*, 2D, 2L
Row 8: Same as Row 7
Row 9: Same as Row 6

Knit in a multiple of five stitches.

Pinwheels

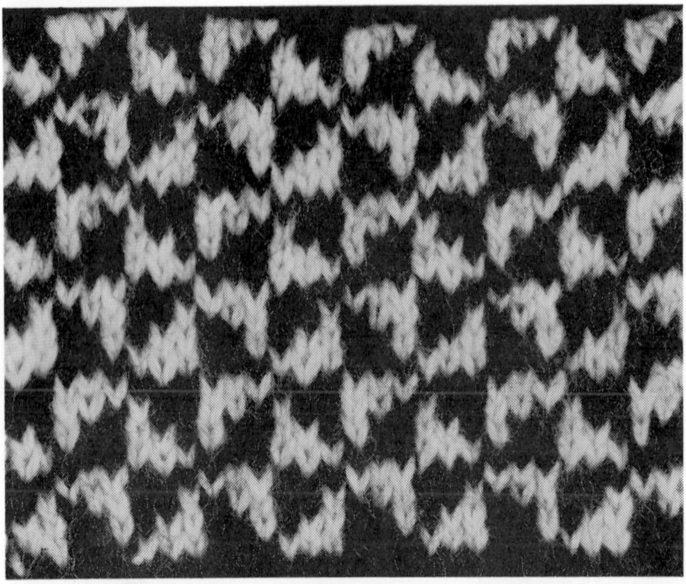

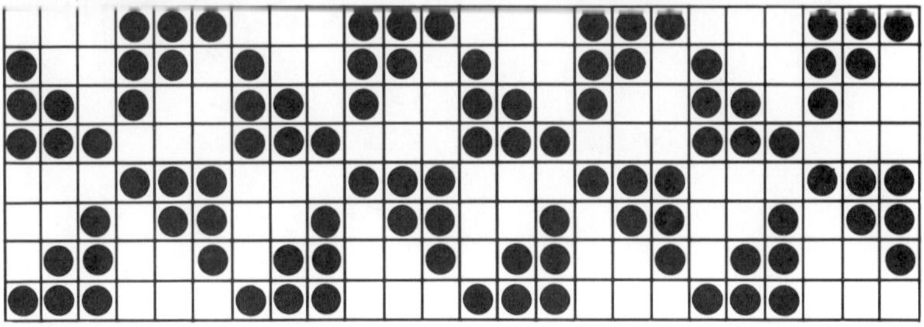

Knit in a multiple of six stitches.

Row 1: k (3L, 3D,)*
Row 2: k (1D, 2L, 2D, 1L)*
Row 3: k (2D, 1L, 1D, 2L)*
Row 4: k (3D, 3L,)*
Row 5: k (3L, 3D)*
Row 6: k (2L, 1D, 1L, 2D)*
Row 7: k (1L, 2D, 2L, 1D)*
Row 8: k (3D, 3L)*

These directions are for knitting in the round. To knit flat pieces, purl even-numbered rows reading the color sequence from right to left.

Sawtooth

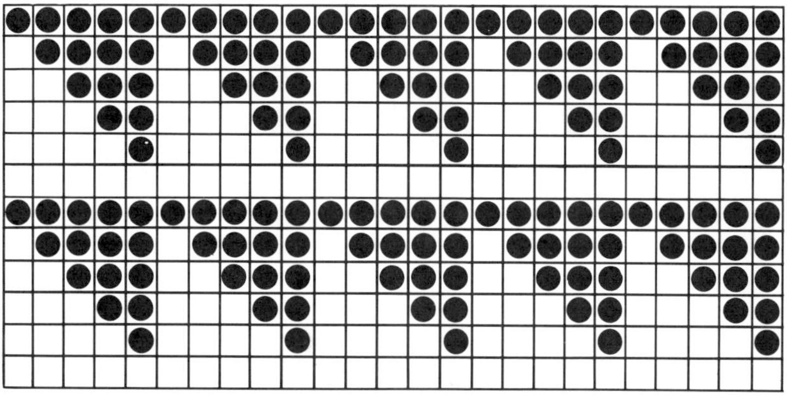

Sawtooth is one of the most common double-knit patterns. The diagram shows a multiple of five stitches, but it may be adapted to four by omitting Row 2, or to three by omitting Rows 2 and 3 for mittens for small children.

Row 1:	k D	Row 1:	k D	Row 1:	k D
Row 2:	k (1L, 4D)*	Row 2:	k 1L, 3D	Row 2:	k 1L, 2D
Row 3:	k (2L, 3D)*	Row 3:	k 2L, 2D	Row 3:	k 2L, 1D
Row 4:	k (3L, 2D)*	Row 4:	k 3L, 1D	Row 4:	k L
Row 5:	k (4L, 1D)*	Row 5:	k L		
Row 6:	k L				

These directions are for knitting in the round. For flat pieces, purl Rows 2, 4, and 6, reading directions for color sequence from right to left.

Sawtooth Variant

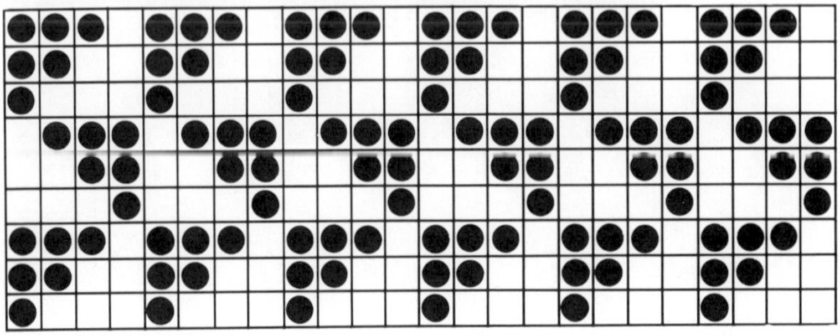

This form of Sawtooth pattern in which the slant of the teeth is changed every other row is used in some parts of Nova Scotia, and also for hunting mitts by Inuit women in Labrador. These mitts have the index finger knit as in a glove. Knit in a multiple of four stiches.

Row 1: k (3D, 1L)*
Row 2: k (2D, 2L)*
Row 3: k (1D, 3L)*
Row 4: k (1L, 3D)*
Row 5: k (2L, 2D)*
Row 6: k (3L, 1D)*

Snail's Trail and Fleur-de-lis

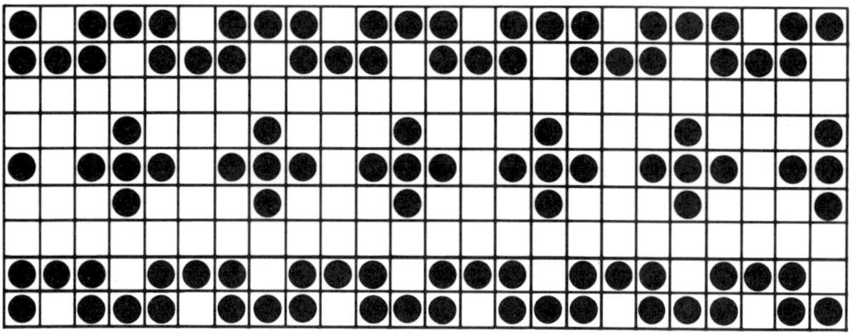

A combination of two old patterns, good for borders or bands on caps, sweaters, etc. Knit in a multiple of four stitches.

Row 1: k 1D, (1L, 3D)*, 1L, 2D
Row 2: k (3D, 1L)* ending with 3D on flat pieces.
Row 3: k L
Row 4: k (3D, 1D)*, ending with 3L on flat pieces.
Row 5: Same as Row 1
Row 6: Same as Row 4
Row 7: Same as Row 3
Row 8: Same as Row 2
Row 9: Same as Row 1

Snow Birds

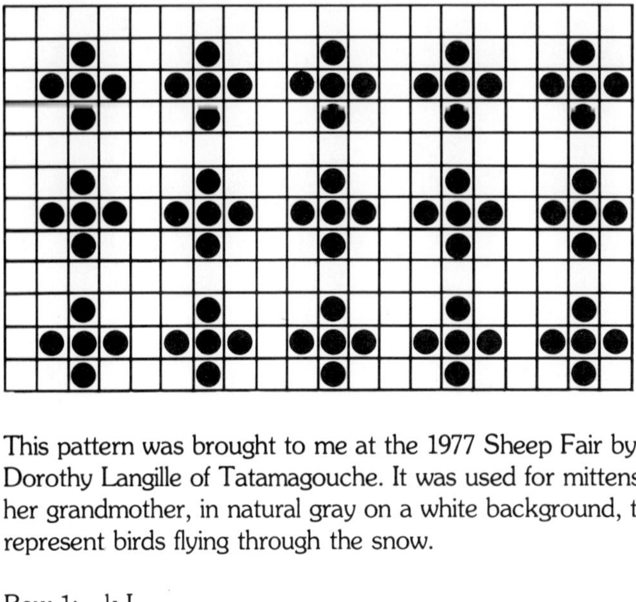

This pattern was brought to me at the 1977 Sheep Fair by Dorothy Langille of Tatamagouche. It was used for mittens by her grandmother, in natural gray on a white background, to represent birds flying through the snow.

Row 1: k L
Row 2: k 2L, (1D, 3L)*, 1D, 2L
Row 3: k 1L, (3D, 1L)*, 3D, 1L
Row 4: Same as Row 2

These four rows are repeated to form the all-over pattern.

Snowflake

This motif is commonly used on the backs of mittens and gloves and in bands on sweaters, in white on a dark colour. Knit in a multiple of twenty-nine stitches.

Row 1: k (5L, 2D, 1L, 2D, 1L, 1D, 1L, 1D, 1L, 1D, 1L, 1D, 1L, 2D, 1L, 2D, 5L)
Row 2: k (1L, 1D, 1L, 1D, 1L, 2D, 2L, 2D, 1L, 1D, 1L, 1D, 1L, 1D, 1L, 2D, 2L, 2D, 1L, 1D, 1L, 1D, 1L)
Row 3: k (5L, 2D, 3L, 2D, 1L, 1D, 1L, 1D, 1L, 2D, 3L, 2D, 5L)
Row 4: k (1L, 1D, 1L, 1D, 1L, 2D, 4L, 2D, 1L, 1D, 1L, 2D, 4L, 2D, 1L, 1D, 1L, 1D, 1L)
Row 5: k (5L, 2D, 5L, 2D, 1L, 2D, 5L, 2D, 5L)
Row 6: k (7D, 6L, 3D, 6L, 7D)
Row 7: k (8D, 6L, 1D, 6L, 8D)
Row 8: k (6L, 3D, 5L, 1D, 5L, 3D, 6L)
Row 9: k (1D, 6L, 3D, 4L, 1D, 4L, 3D, 6L, 1D)
Row 10: k (2D, 6L, 3D, 3L, 1D, 3L, 3D, 6L, 2D)
Row 11: k (1L, 2D, 6L, 3D, 2L, 1D, 2L, 3D, 6L, 2D, 1L)
Row 12: k (1D, 1L, 2D, 6L, 3D, 1L, 1D, 1L, 3D, 6L, 2D, 1L, 1D)

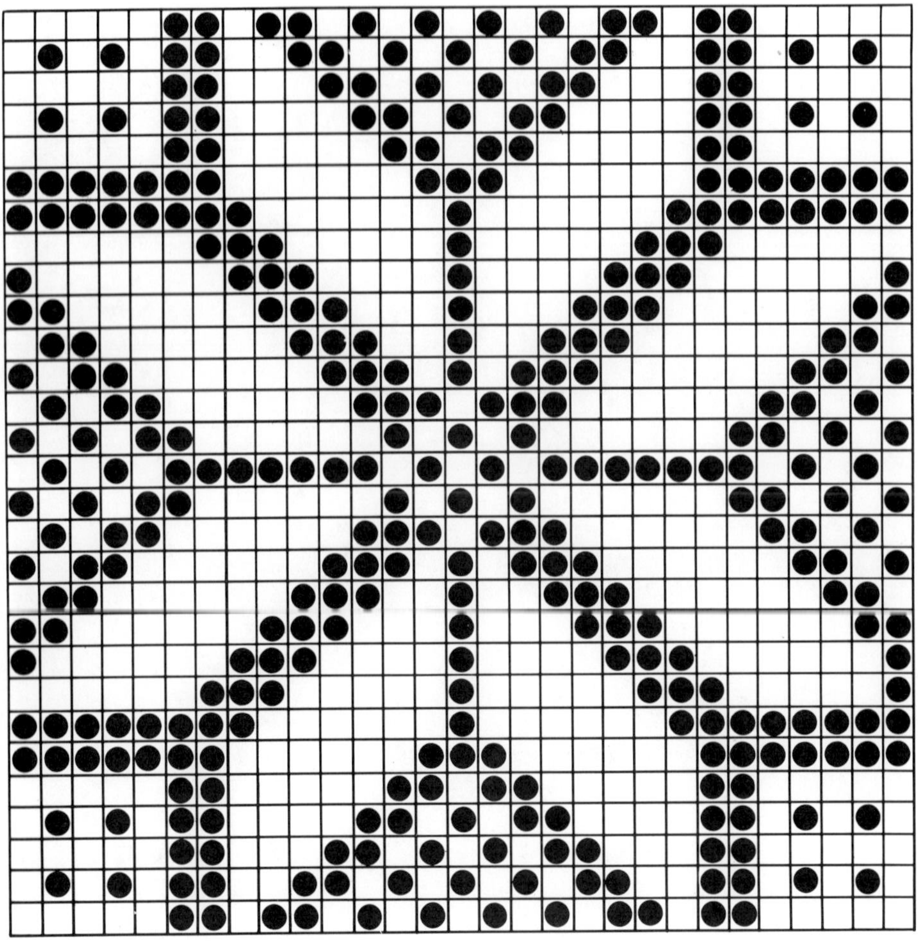

Row 13: k (1L, 1D, 1L, 2D, 6L, 3D, 1L, 3D, 6L, 2D, 1L, 1D, 1L)
Row 14: k (1D, 1L, 1D, 1L, 2D, 6L, 1D, 1L, 1D, 1L, 1D, 6L, 2D, 1L, 1D, 1L, 1D)
Row 15: k (1L, 1D, 1L, 1D, 1L, 7D, 1L, 1D, 1L, 1D, 1L, 7D, 1L, 1D, 1L, 1D, 1L)

Row 15 the centre of the motif. Work Rows 14 to 1 in reverse to complete motif.

Windowpane

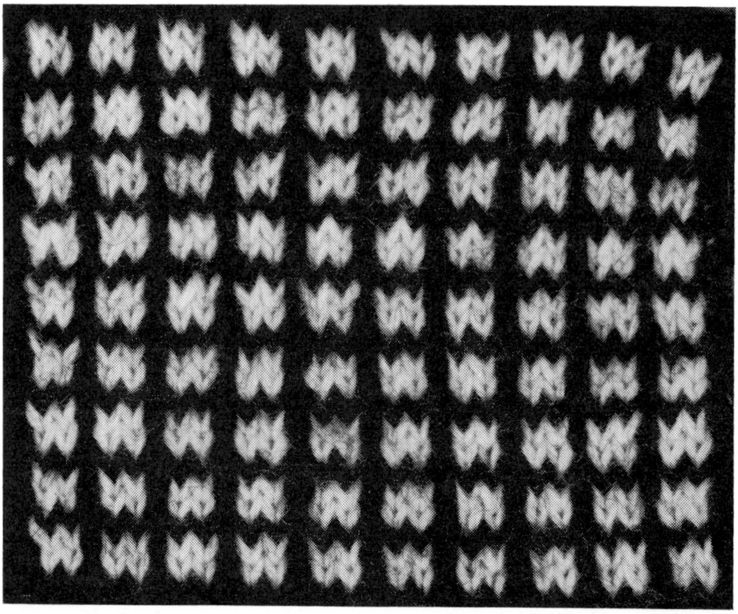

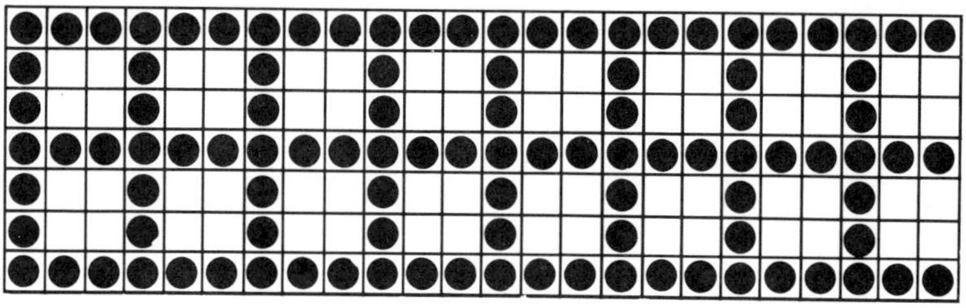

This is another very common pattern which may be adapted to various size panes. The directions are for a multiple of three stitches (plus one to balance in flat knitting).

Row 1: k D
Row 2: k (1D, 2L)*
Row 3: Same as Row 2

These directions are for knitting in the round. For flat pieces, purl Row 2 ending with 1D. Proceed with:

Row 4: p D
Row 5: k as Row 2
Row 6: p as Row 2

Zig-Zag

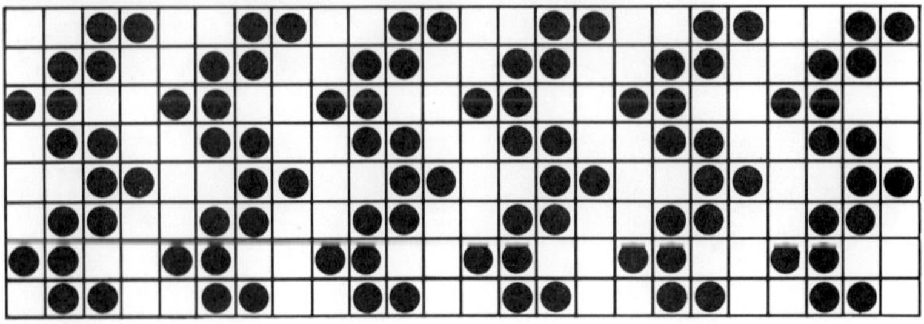

This is a very old pattern used for mittens, gloves, caps, and sometimes sweaters. It is knit in a multiple of four stitches.

Row 1: k (2L, 2D)*
Row 2: k 1L, (2D, 2L)* 2D, 1L
Row 3: k (2D, 2L)*
Row 4: Same as Row 2

These directions are for knitting in the round. For flat knitting, purl Rows 2 and 4, reading color sequence from right to left.